STRATEGIES IN LISTENING

TASKS FOR LISTENING DEVELOPMENT

NEW EDITION

Michael Rost
Munetsugu Uruno

LINGUAL HOUSE

Published by

Longman Asia ELT
A division of Addison Wesley Longman
2nd Floor, Cornwall House
Taikoo Place
979 King's Road
Quarry Bay
Hong Kong
fax: +852 2856 9578
e-mail: aelt@awl.com.hk

http://www.awl-elt.com

Longman Japan KK
1-13-19 Sekiguchi
Bunkyo-ku
Tokyo 112
Japan
fax: +81 3 3266 0326

and Associated Companies throughout the world

This book was developed for Longman Asia ELT by Lateral Communications Limited. Lingual House is an imprint of Longman Asia ELT.

Produced by Longman Asia Limited, Hong Kong
SWTC/04

Developmental Editor:	Michael Rost
Content Editor:	Anne McGannon
Project Coordinator:	Keiko Kimura
Cover Design:	Kotaro Kato
Text Design:	Keiko Kimura
Text Design Advisor:	Georgia Kalnin
Cover Illustration:	Shozo Yanagimoto
Text Illustrations:	Kiyoshi Ishikawa, Mark Ziemann, Miriam Fabbri
Recording Supervision:	David Joslyn

Acknowledgements

We would like to thank the following teachers who provided valuable suggestions for the revision of *Strategies in Listening*:

Won-Key Lee
Keith Lane
Chris Deziel
Mary Catlett
Meiho Chiu

Christopher Deziel
Yasuyuki Ikeshima
Noriko Kochi
Jean Mackay
Akie Matsui

ISBN Textbook 962 00 1033 7 Manual 962 00 1034 5 Cassette 962 00 1035 3 CDs 962 00 1036 1

5 4 3

The
publisher's
policy is to use
**paper manufactured
from sustainable forests**

INTRODUCTION

Strategies in Listening is designed to help students of English from beginner through intermediate level to develop the listening skills needed for natural conversation. The course exposes students to a variety of discourse situations, speaking styles, and listening tasks and helps them learn strategies for understanding American English conversation. The listening extracts in *Strategies in Listening* are challenging, but all are presented with a clearly structured task that enables students to deal with authentic conversations and extended passages.

The book consists of 18 units which are to be used with the accompanying set of audio materials (cassettes or CDs). Each unit is organized around a theme — the units progress from tangible themes to more abstract themes.

• The first section of each unit, **Get Ready,** is a preview that highlights important ideas and language that will help the students with the upcoming listening tasks. The **Idea Preview** activates students' knowledge and stimulates opinions related to the topic of the unit. The **Langauge Preview** highlights important words and expressions that will help the students understand the upcoming conversations.

• The second section of each unit is a series of three listening tasks (A ,B, C) which encourage students to focus on the meaning of the extracts, rather than try to comprehend and recall everything they hear. These tasks emphasize predicting, making inferences, and problem solving.

• The third section of each unit is called the **Pair Activity**. This is a short activity that the students perform in pairs. By working on these tasks, the students will create important links between conversational listening and speaking.

Two special features of *Strategies in Listening* are:

• Strategy Check Units that present and review 12 essential strategies in listening.

• Review Tests, which allow teachers to check student progress and provide students an opportunity to review listening skills and strategies.

TAPES/CDs

Strategies in Listening is accompanied by a set of audio **cassettes** (or **CD**s). The tapes are recorded to simulate authentic speech. Tape scripts are available in the **Teacher's Manual**. The **Teacher's Manual** also contains classroom teaching suggestions.

CONTENTS

CONTENTS

Get Ready

Idea Preview

What's your first name? ....

What's your last name? ....

Do you have a middle name? ....

What title do you use? (Mr., Ms., Dr., Professor) ....

Professor	Janice	Lynn	Smith	"Jan"	JLS
title	first name (given name)	middle name	last name	nickname	initials

Language Preview

Do you know these words?

line   box   check   circle   top   bottom   right   left

"Excuse me"   "Pardon me"   "Fill out..."

A Here are some simple instructions. Listen and follow the instructions.

1.

_____

2.

3.

4.

5.

6.

_____

_____

B Listen and follow the instructions.

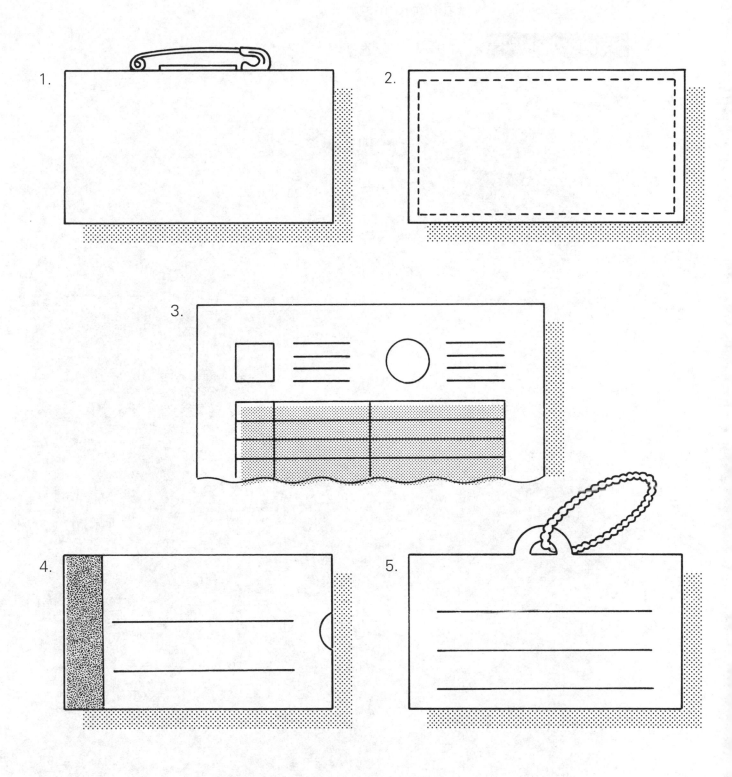

1.

2.

3.

4.

5.

Compare your answers with your classmate.

C Do you have a video club card? Did you fill out an application?
Tiffany Johnson is filling out an application with her dad.
Listen and write down the information.

LISTENING STRATEGY   Predict what the speakers will say.

MEMBERSHIP APPLICATION

STREETBUSTER VIDEO

2001 University St.
Berkeley, CA 94601

....

....

....

....

OFFICE USE ONLY

STREETBUSTER
MEMBER #

APPROVAL CODE

SECURITY TYPE
Circle one of the following:
    VISA   MASTERCARD   AMEX
SECONDARY ID TYPE
If you do not carry one of the credit cards listed above, enter a secondary ID type. A one-time processing fee will
be charged to your account when you use a secondary ID type. ....
ID type ....

ADDITIONAL FAMILY MEMBERS
Please indicate the names of others who are authorized by Applicant to rent video tapes, games and related
equipment on this STREETBUSTER VIDEO CLUB MEMBERSHIP.

NUMBER OF CARDS REQUESTED

STREETBUSTER Policy is to refuse rental or sale of "R" and "YRV" rated videos to youths under the age of 17,
unless parental consent is given.
Please check one of the following:
1. DO NOT ALLOW children listed on my membership application to rent or buy "R" or "YRV" rated videos.
2. ALLOW children listed on my membership application to rent or buy "R" or "YRV" rated videos.

Parent signature ....

P air A ctivity

D Work with a partner. Give your partner instructions. Use expressions like these:

Write your name on the top line.
Write your address in the box.
Write your phone number under the line.
Write your favorite food on the left.

Get Ready

Language Preview

Match each function with one expression.

introduce	"I'm sorry. I forgot."
greet	"This isn't really hot enough."
welcome	"Hey, that's great!"
congratulate	"I think Tokyo is a beautiful city."
apologize	"Hi. How are you today?"
invite	"I'm Mari. Glad to meet you."
request	"Would you like to come along?"
request permission	"Can I have two coffees, please?"
suggest	"Why don't you take the subway?"
warn	"Be careful. That's heavy."
complain	"Come in. Have a seat."
give an opinion	"Can I join you?"

Now listen and check your answers.
Can you think of one more expression for each function?

A Here are some common expressions. Listen. Complete the sentences.

1. I'd like you .... my husband, Kenji.

2. Oh, gosh. ....

3. This is .... It's too ....

4. You'd ....

5. .... a beer, please.

6. Why .... you ....?

Now listen again and check your answers.

B Here are some conversations with simple functions. Can you understand what the speakers are doing? Listen and write the function next to the picture.

introducing   greeting   thanking   congratulating   suggesting
apologizing   offering   requesting   saying good-bye   request permission

1 ....

2 ....

3 ....

4 ....

5 ....

6 ....

7 ....

8 ....

C   Here are some things that people often say.   Listen. How would you respond?
Write a short answer.

LISTENING STRATEGY   Give a quick response.

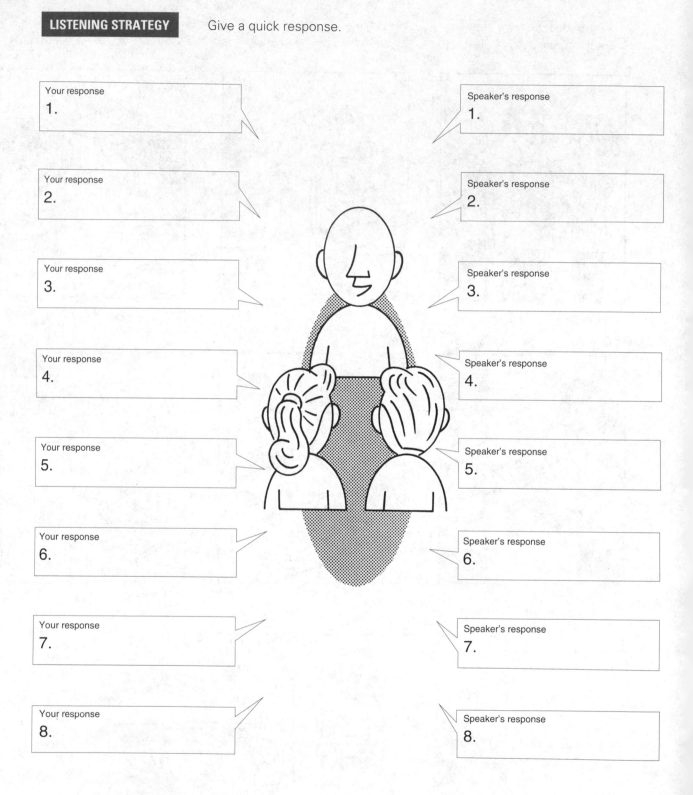

Your response
1.

Your response
2.

Your response
3.

Your response
4.

Your response
5.

Your response
6.

Your response
7.

Your response
8.

Speaker's response
1.

Speaker's response
2.

Speaker's response
3.

Speaker's response
4.

Speaker's response
5.

Speaker's response
6.

Speaker's response
7.

Speaker's response
8.

Now listen. What do they say? Write their responses.

Pair Activity

D Choose a card 1-5. Together, make a short conversation.
Try again with another card.

1. APOLOGY
Boss and employee

2. CONGRATULATIONS
Two friends

3. THANKING
Two friends

4. WISHING GOOD LUCK
Teacher and student

5. OFFERING
Two friends

Now make up two original situations.
Act them out in front of the class.
Can the class guess:
What is happening?
Who are the people?

Get Ready

Idea Preview

Look at each picture. Where is it? What is happening?

1.    2.    3.    4.

5.    6.    7.    8.

Now listen.

Language Preview

Where can you hear these expressions?   Do you know these words?

Can I help you?   embarrassed   upset
The doctor will be right with you.   angry   sorry
How much will that be?
It's your turn.

A   Listen to these sequences. Where are they? What is happening?
Write your answers.

1. Where are they?

   What is happening?

2. Where are they?

   What is happening?

3. Where are they?

   What is happening?

4. Where are they?

   What is happening?

Compare your answers with a classmate. Are your answers the same?

Here are some unusual situations.
Can you guess what happened? How do the speakers feel? Write your answers.

LISTENING STRATEGY   Think about the situation.

1.

What happened?

How does Mr. Carter feel?
a. embarrassed
b. excited

2.

What happened?

How does the man feel?
a. sorry
b. angry

3.

What happened?

How does he feel?
a. happy
b. nervous

4.

What happened?

How does she feel?
a. she likes him
b. she doesn't like him

5.

What happened?

How does she feel?
a. angry
b. scared

6.

What happened?

How does she feel?
a. sorry
b. upset

Compare your answers with a classmate. Are your answers the same?

Pair Activity

D Read these short conversations out loud. Partner A, say the A line.
Partner B, say the B line. What's the situation? Think of two possibilities.

1.
ANYTHING ELSE?

NO, THAT'S ALL.

1.
2.

2.
THANKS FOR SEEING ME TODAY.

NO PROBLEM. WHAT CAN I DO FOR YOU.

1.
2.

3.
THIS PLACE IS A MESS. DID YOU USE THIS?

DON'T WORRY... I'LL CLEAN IT UP.

1.
2.

4.
HURRY UP! WE'RE WAITING FOR YOU.

OK, OK, I'LL BE THERE IN A MINUTE.

1.
2.

5.
ARE YOU COMING TOMORROW?

YES. DON'T WORRY. I'LL BE THERE.

1.
2.

6.
WHAT WOULD YOU LIKE?

NOTHING ELSE. BRING ME THE CHECK PLEASE.

1.
2.

CHECK UNIT

LISTENING STRATEGIES: Part One

Let's review three strategies for listening.

STRATEGY 1: Don't worry about unclear sounds.
You will often be surprised when you listen to spoken English. That's OK! Many sounds in spoken English are not very clear.
Don't worry — you don't need to hear every sound.

Here are two examples. Which words are not clear? Circle them.

1. He must have seen you.   2. Can you do it for me?

STRATEGY 2: Think about the situation.
Sometimes you will have difficulty understanding English.
Don't panic! Think about the situation.
The situation will give you information to help you understand.

Here are two examples. What question do you think the person is asking?

1. You're at the airport. You're checking in for an international flight.
   Airline agent: .... passport?

2. You're at a department store. You put something on the counter to buy.
   Clerk: .... credit card?

STRATEGY 3: Ask if you don't understand.
You will have a lot of questions when you listen. That's good!
Don't be afraid to ask questions.
Asking questions will help you understand better.

Here are two examples. Complete the questions that the listener asks.

1. A: Use a spatula.   B: .... spatula?

2. A: Please do the bottom of page 44   B: .... 44 and 45?
      and the top of 45.

Get Ready

Language Preview

Do you know these words?

shirts and blouses: long-sleeve, short-sleeve
sweaters: V-neck, crew neck, turtleneck
skirts: long, tight
pants: straight leg, sweat pants, shorts
jackets and coats: top coat, jacket, baseball jacket
suits: two-piece, three-piece
foreign dress: sari, kimono
patterns: solid, checked, striped, plaid

Work with a partner. Look at three students in your class.
Describe their clothes.

.... is wearing..

Now look at three different students. Describe where they are and
what they're doing.

.... is sitting next to the door. She is talking to.............................

A Here are some group pictures. What kind of groups are they?
Listen. Match the names with the people in the picture.

1.

2.

Rose   Gail   Jay   Roy   Sonny   Val   Bonnie   Anthony

3.

Little John   Banger   Slug Face   Willy the Loner   Blimp

Compare your answers with a classmate. Are your answers the same?

B Some of these people look very similar. Listen. Who are they talking about? Write the number of the conversation next to the correct picture.

....

....

C Each person was asked this question:
"Are you attractive to people of the opposite sex?" What did they answer?

LISTENING STRATEGY   Ask if you don't understand.

1. Stan

his answer
............*yes/no*...............
Why?

2. Marsha

her answer
............*yes/no*...............
Why?

3. Jon

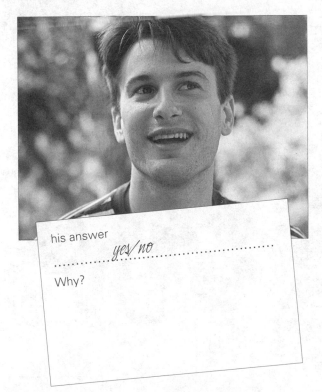

his answer
............*yes/no*...............
Why?

4. Rachel

her answer
............*yes/no*...............
Why?

21

Pair Activity

D Partner 1, look only at Picture A. Cover up Picture B.
Partner 2, look only at Picture B. Cover up Picture A.

Describe the people. Can your partner find them in his or her picture?

HINT
Describe clothes and appearance.

22

5 MESSAGES

Get Ready

Idea Preview

Do you have an answering machine?
Do you ever take messages for other people? For whom?
Do you mind taking messages?

Language Preview

Here is how we can say telephone numbers in English:

The number is 313 - 479 - 3077 x 21
                (area code)   (extension)

Here is how we can ask for information:

Can you tell me the number of Michelle Adams?
Do you have a listing for Michelle Adams?
I need the number of Michelle Adams.

A We often call "information" when we don't know a phone number.
Listen to these calls. Write the correct phone number.

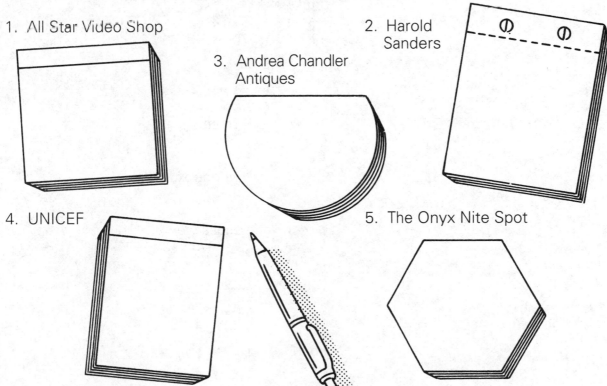

1. All Star Video Shop

2. Harold Sanders

3. Andrea Chandler Antiques

4. UNICEF

5. The Onyx Nite Spot

B Do you have an answering machine? Do you get a lot of messages?
Listen to Mike's messages. Write them down.

1.

from:
   Bill

phone number:

message:
   call him

2.

from:

phone number:

message:

3.

from:

message:

4.

from:

phone number:

message:

C Here are some conversations about times and places.
Fill in the information as you listen.

LISTENING STRATEGY   Guess the speaker's meaning.

1. American Embassy

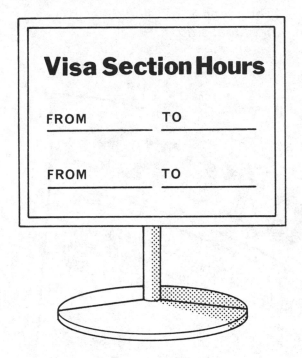

Visa Section Hours

FROM _____   TO _____

FROM _____   TO _____

2. a date

MEET
AT _____ (TIME)
AT _____ (PLACE)

3. an appointment

CHANGE

FROM _____ AT _____
(DAY)   (TIME)

TO _____ AT _____
(DAY)   (TIME)

4. a meeting

MEET
ON _____ (DAY)
AT _____ (TIME)

D Partner 1, you are an information operator.
Partner 2, you need four phone numbers.
Make a conversation like this:

A: Excuse me, I need the number for Harlan Sanderson.
A: Yes.
A: 775-3709?
A: Thank you.

B: *Did you say Harlan Sanderson?*

B: *The number is 775-3709.*
B: *Yes, that's right.*

Partner 1, use the information below.

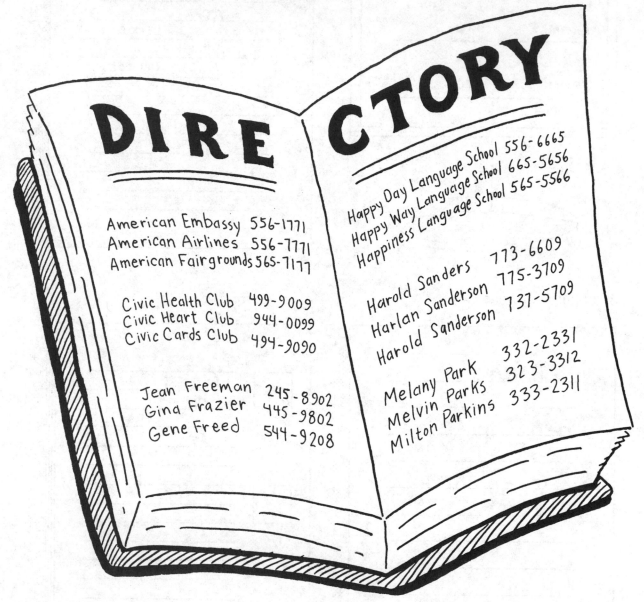

DIRE CTORY

American Embassy   556-1771
American Airlines   556-7771
American Fairgrounds 565-7177

Civic Health Club   499-9009
Civic Heart Club   944-0099
Civic Cards Club   494-9090

Jean Freeman   245-8902
Gina Frazier   445-9802
Gene Freed   544-9208

Happy Day Language School 556-6665
Happy Way Language School 665-5656
Happiness Language School 565-5566

Harold Sanders   773-6609
Harlan Sanderson   775-3709
Harold Sanderson   737-5709

Melany Park   332-2331
Melvin Parks   323-3312
Milton Parkins   333-2311

Now switch roles and try again.

6 PLANS

Get Ready

Idea Preview

Holiday plans: Do you have any plans for the next holiday?
                           What are you going to do?

Invitations: Has anyone invited you to an event recently?
                           Who invited you?
                           Where did you go?

A   Listen to these people talking about their plans. Fill in the charts.

1. Martin and Megumi are talking about their holidays.

	last holiday	next holiday
Martin		
Megumi		

2. Alice and Patrick are talking about their weekend plans.

	last weekend	this weekend
Alice		
Patrick		

3. Michael and Simon are talking about their evening activities.

	last night	tonight
Michael		
Simon		

Listen again. What verb forms do they use? Complete the sentences.

1. Martin, what .... on your last holiday?

I went to............................ .

2. Patrick, what are you .... to do this weekend?

I'm not sure. I think .... to the Blind Lemon concert.

3. Simon, ... you at home last night?

Yeah, I .... I .... get ready for a big test.

Compare your answers with a classmate.

B Here are some invitations. Listen. What is the invitation for?
Fill in the blanks. Does the second person accept or not? Circle yes or no.

invitation to ....   accept?

1. Masu's .... on ....   Y   N

2. .... at Heather Park on ....   Y   N

3. .... at Wendy's house on ....   Y   N

4. .... in the Sierra Mountains next ....   Y   N

5. .... at NHK Hall on ....   Y   N

C Three couples are talking about their vacation plans.
Listen to each conversation. What places are they considering?
Where do they decide to go?

LISTENING STRATEGY   Pay attention to stressed words.

1. Margo and Phil

considering:

.... and ....

They decide to go to

....

reason

....

considering:

.... and ....

They decide to go to

....

reason

....

2. Eric and Louise

3. Jamie and Allen

considering:

.... and ....

They decide to go to

....

reason

....

D What do you like to do to when you go on a short holiday?
Rank your five favorite activities. (1-5)

Compare your list with your partner. Give reasons.

Describe a recent trip. Say at least 5 things about it.

Let's review three strategies for listening.

STRATEGY 4: Pay attention to stressed words.
When you listen to English, you notice that some words have strong stress.
Pay attention to these words!
Understanding stressed words helps you follow the conversation.

> Here is an example conversation. Which words are stressed? Underline them.
>
> A: What's your teacher like? B: *Oh, she's very interesting and she always talks a lot.*
>   *I think she's very friendly.*

STRATEGY 5: Guess the speaker's meaning.
When you listen to English, you will hear many new words and expressions. Don't worry—
that's normal! Try to guess the general meaning. The general meaning is usually all you need.

> Here are two examples. Which words are unfamiliar? Can you guess the meaning?
>
> Please come to dinner at seven o'clock. It's very nice weather today, so we'll be eating dinner
> on the veranda.
>
> veranda probably means ....
>
> I'm going to serve some exquisite food. I learned to make a delicious dish when I was
> living in Thailand.
>
> exquisite probably means ....

STRATEGY 6: Give a quick response.
Sometimes when we listen, we get confused or embarrassed. We don't want
to say anything. Try to say something — even if you're not sure.
When you respond quickly, you will feel more confident about listening.

> Here are some ways to respond:
> (a) give short answers   (b) ask a question   (c) make a statement about you
> Here are three examples. How does the listener (Tom) respond — a, b, or c?
>
> 1. Lisa: Let's go to Ajanta for dinner.   Tom: *No, I don't want to eat Indian food today.* ☐
>
> 2. Lisa: I'm going to the Computer Center.   Tom: *Sorry? Where?* ☐
>
> 3. Lisa: How are you doing today?   Tom: *OK.* ☐

Get Ready

Idea Preview

Can you give instructions for...

using a CD player?
checking in at an airline counter?
starting a car?
checking books out of a library?

Language Preview

Listen. Complete these sentences:

1. I'm .... tell you .... do this.

2. ...., you have to ....

3. .... to show your ticket...

4. .... put the books on the counter.

A Look at the pictures. Imagine the situation.
What kind of instructions is the person giving? Number the pictures.

....

....

....

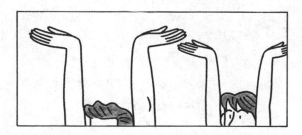

....

Listen again. Put the steps in order. Write 1, 2, 3, 4.

B Do you sometimes make mistakes? Here are some mistakes.
Listen to the instructions. What's wrong? Try to correct the mistakes.

Compare your answers with a classmate. Are your answers the same?

C **Do you know these games? Read some of the basic rules.**

LISTENING STRATEGY   Predict what the speakers will say.

Pass the Orange
- Stand in a line.
- The first person in each line gets an orange.
- Place the orange under your chin.

Kim's Game
- Collect 20 or 30 objects.
- Put them on a tray and then you cover it with a cloth.
- Remove the cloth, for 30 seconds.

Charades
- Divide the players into two teams.
- Choose a movie title or song title.
- Try to act out the title.

Achi
- Each player starts with nine colored stones.
- Take turns. Try to place your stones in a line.

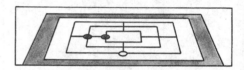

Pachinko
- You play at a machine.
- Try to make the balls go into the targets.

Now listen. Which game are they describing? Number the pictures.

KEY WORDS

- stand in a line
- tuck it under your chin
- gather around
- remove the cloth
- sort of a party game
- use signals and gestures
- concentric square
- take a turn
- different targets
- object of the game

Compare your answers with a classmate. Are your answers the same?

D Choose one of the activities below.
Partner 1, give step-by-step instructions how to do it. Use at least 5 actions.
Partner 2, mime the actions.

Example: • wash your face

1. Turn on the water.
2. Put your hands together.
3. Scoop some water into your hands.
4. Throw the water on your face.
5. Rub your face with your hands.
6. Pick up a towel.
7. Dry your face.

Now choose one of these actions.

making a green salad

making a phone call

starting a car

changing a flat tire

ordering food in a restaurant

writing a letter on a computer

buying a ticket for a train

cooking rice

getting on a bus

changing the battery in a Walkman

Now switch roles. Try again.

Get Ready

Language Preview

Do you know these expressions?

APPEARANCE
GENERAL: attractive   good-looking   average-looking   not very good-looking
HEIGHT: tall   short   average height
BODY TYPE: heavy   medium build   thin/slim/slender
HAIR: long   short   straight   curly   wavy   thin   bald

PERSONALITY
serious   funny   warm   open   nice   shy
quiet   loud   outgoing   nervous   smart (intelligent)
thoughtful   kind   mean   bossy   polite   rude
optimistic   pessimistic

Think of one famous person.

Name: ....

Describe this person. Use some of the expressions above.

....

....

A Listen. How do they describe each person?
Write two expressions for each person.

1. a bank robber
    body type   hair

2. a fiancée
    appearance   height

3. a boss
    body type   clothes

4.

a son

age   accessories

5.

an English teacher

body type   clothes

Compare your answers with a classmate. Are your answers similar?

B Lee and Anita are brother and sister. Listen to them describe the people in their family. Write one expression for each person.

	Lee	Anita
Father	....	....
Mother	....	....
Lee	....	....
Anita	....	....

Listen again. What do they like about each person?

	Lee	Anita
Father	....	....
Mother	....	....
Lee		....
Anita	....	

C Do you know these famous people? Listen. Who are they describing? Write the number next to the correct name.

LISTENING STRATEGY Focus on key words.

...... Nicole Kidman, movie star

...... Barbra Streisand, singer

...... Kurt Cobain, musician

...... Albert Einstein, physicist

...... Steven Spielberg, director

...... Gloria Steinem, writer

Pair Activity

D On your own, write the names of 3 famous people.

1. .... 2. .... 3. ....

Wesley Snipes

Whoopi Goldberg

Shaquille O'Neal

Princess Diana

Daniel Day-Lewis

Bruce Springsteen

Nelson Mandela

Madonna

Michael Bolton

Yoko Ono

Barbra Streisand

Woody Allen

Now choose one name. Your partner will try to guess your famous person. Your partner can ask only 10 yes/no questions.

Example: OK

Is she American?
Do we see her often?
Did she write books?

NOT OK

What's her nationality?
When do we see her?
What did she do?

Now switch roles. Try again.

A Instructions (15 points)
Listen and fill out the application.

MEMBERSHIP APPLICATION

STREETBUSTER VIDEO

2133 Main St.
Albany, NY 21108

OFFICE USE ONLY

....

....

....

....

STREETBUSTER
MEMBER #

APPROVAL CODE

B Messages (20 points)
Fill in the information as you listen.

1. Hillary Sanders ....
2. Brent Chandler Antiques ....
3. Appointment time .... phone ....
4. New appointment time .... day ....

C Situations (10 points)
Listen. Where are they ? Circle the answer.

1. a. department store
   b. grocery store
   c. restaurant

2. a. at home
   b. in a classsroom
   c. in a shop

3. a. at the post office
   b. at a department store
   c. at a restaurant

4. a. at school
   b. at the doctor's office
   c. in the teacher's office

5. a. in a classroom
   b. in the teacher's office
   c. at the office

6. a. at a concert
   b. at a shop
   c. at home

D Functions (10 points)
Listen. Which sentence or question has the same meaning? Circle the answer.

1. a. May I borrow your pen?
   b. Here. Use my pen.
   c. Do you have my pen?

2. a. I'll clean it up.
   b. You should clean it up.
   c. Let's clean it up together.

3. a. Please hurry.
   b. I'm sorry I'm late.
   c. Where were you?

4. a. Would you like to come along?
   b. Can I come with you?
   c. Where are you going?

5. a. Glad to meet you.
   b. This is Harry Jones.
   c. I'd like to meet him.

6. a. I don't like this.
   b. This is great.
   c. Would you like some?

7. a. Do you want some coffee?
   b. Do you want one or two?
   c. I'd like two coffees.

8. a. You should take the subway.
   b. Don't take the subway.
   c. Why are you taking the subway?

9. a. This is really hot.
   b. This is warm, not hot.
   c. This is hot enough.

10. a. I'm sorry about the meeting.
    b. I was on time for the meeting.
    c. The meeting was yesterday.

E Reasons (15 points)
Listen to each conversation. What are they going to do? Why?
Circle the answer.

1. They're going to .... because ....
   a. go to Mexico   a. they like to swim
   b. go to Hawaii   b. they would like to visit relatives.
   c. go to Thailand   c. they want to save money

2. They're going to .... because ....
   a. play tennis   a. it's so hot.
   b. go swimming   b. they have to clean the house.
   c. stay at home   c. they don't have any free time.

3. He's going to .... New York because ....
   a. visit   a. he found a new job
   b. move to   b. he enjoys traveling
   c. leave   c. he wants to visit his family

F Descriptions (15 points)
Listen. Write the correct name under each person.

Gene

Emmet

Bella

Celia

Sidney

G Processes (15 points)
Listen. Put the steps in order.

1.

....

2.

....

3.

....

What is your score for this review test? [   ] / [   ] %
100 points

Self Evaluation

Look at page 18 and page 31.
Which strategies are helping you listen better?

....
....
....

Which strategies do you want to try using more?

....
....
....

Get Ready

Idea Preview

Can you solve this problem?
Put the numbers 1-9 in each box so that the total of each line is 15.

The "magic square"

$$\square + 9 + 4 = 15$$

$$7 + \square + \square = 15$$

$$\square + 1 + \square = 15$$

15 15 15

Now listen and check.

A Look at these figures. What do you see? Compare answers with a partner.

1.

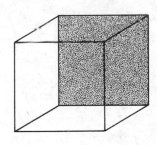

.... or ....

2.

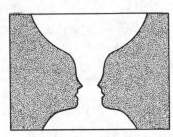

.... or ....

3.

.... or ....

4.

.... or ....

5.

.... or ....

Now listen. What are the two possible answers?

B Do you like figure problems? Listen. First just describe the problem.

1. The coins

How can you move only .... and make the arrow point ....?

2. The nine dots and the four lines

How can you .... all nine dots using only ....?

3. The six glasses

Change the line so that no .... is next to another .... and no .... is next to another.................................

4. The gardener and the four trees

How should the gardener plant the trees so that ....
....?

KEY WORDS

1.
• form an arrow
• in the opposite direction

2.
• arranged in three rows
• connect all nine dots.

3.
• full
• empty
• so that no empty glass is...

4.
• the same distance apart

Now listen for clues to the puzzles. Write the clues.

1. The coins

....
....
....

2. The nine dots and the four lines

....
....
....

3. The six glasses

....
....
....

4. The gardener and the four trees

....
....
....

Now listen one more time. What is the solution?

1.   The coins

2.   The nine dots and the four lines

• • •

• • •

• • •

3. The six glasses

4.   The gardener and the four trees

C   Do you like "Brain Teasers"?   These are logic problems that have unusual solutions.   Let's try a few!   What is the problem?

1. Mr. Higgins

Why does Mr. Higgins ....
.... ?

2. John and Mary

How did John and Mary ....
....?

3.   The man in the rain

Why didn't ....?

4.   The nameless person

Everyone knew who she was, but nobody knew her ....   Why not?

Listen again. What are the solutions?

1. Mr. Higgins

....

....

2. John and Mary

....

....

3. The man in the rain

....

....

4. The nameless person

....

....

KEY WORDS

1.
- apartment building
- press the button
- ground floor
- walks up to...

2.
- found dead
- middle of...
- broken glass
- no blood

3.
- went for a walk
- got wet

P air A ctivity

D Can your partner solve these puzzles? What comes next?

Riddles and jokes: Can you think of any riddles or jokes to tell your partner?
Does your partner understand?
Choose the best riddles and jokes in the class. Write them on the board.

Get Ready

Idea Preview

Look at these occupations. Choose three that you would like. Rank them 1, 2, 3.
Then compare your list with a partner. Give a reason why you chose each job.

architect	doctor	journalist	sales representative
cook	engineer	fashion model	high school teacher
dentist	carpenter	airline pilot	computer programmer
professor	hairdresser	police officer	graphic designer

Example:
I'd like to be a carpenter because you get to work with your hands.
I'd like to be a carpenter because I could work with my hands.

Now choose one job that you would not like. Explain why.

A   What do you think is important in a job? Check your answers.

	Very Important	Somewhat Important	Not So Important
work with people	☐	☐	☐
work by yourself	☐	☐	☐
make a lot of money	☐	☐	☐
make just enough money	☐	☐	☐
enjoy your job	☐	☐	☐
work for a successful company	☐	☐	☐
learn a lot from your job	☐	☐	☐
have a challenging job	☐	☐	☐
have a simple job	☐	☐	☐

B Now listen to Alan, Bart, and Carole. What's important for them?
Check the correct boxes.

Very Important

1. Alan
   work with interesting people ☐
   work by yourself ☐

2. Bart
   make a lot of money ☐
   have an exciting job ☐

3. Carole
   enjoy your job ☐
   work for a successful company ☐
   learn a lot from your job ☐

Listen. What are their reasons? Complete these sentences.

1.   2.   3.

Alan says that he wants to
....
....
And he thinks that your job
has to be ....

Bart thinks that work is your
....
....,
so it's important to get a job
with ....
....

Carole thinks that since
work is the ....
.... *in your life,*
you have to ....
....

Listen to these people talking about their jobs. What do they do?
Write your answers.

LISTENING STRATEGY   Try to understand the speaker's purpose.

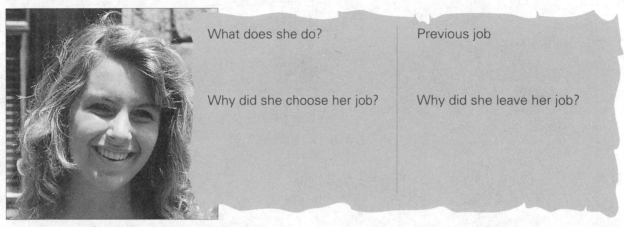

What does she do?	Previous job
Why did she choose her job?	Why did she leave her job?

Carla

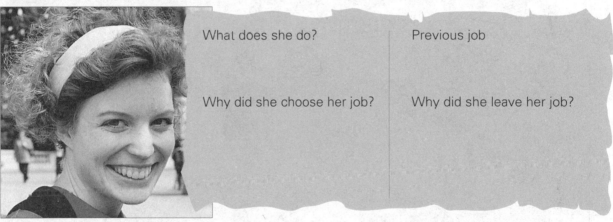

What does she do?	Previous job
Why did she choose her job?	Why did she leave her job?

Angie

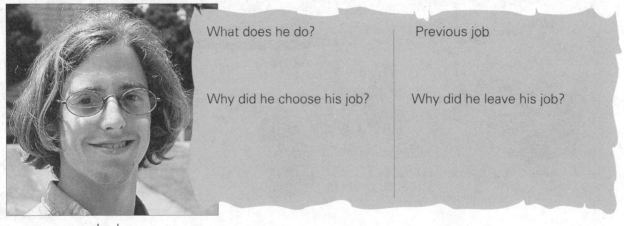

What does he do?	Previous job
Why did he choose his job?	Why did he leave his job?

Jack

Listen again. What were their previous jobs?
Why did they leave their previous jobs?

Pair Activity

D What's important to you in a job? Choose two items that are important and two items that are not important.

Now talk about your choices with a partner.

Let's review three more strategies for listening.

STRATEGY 7: Try to understand the speaker's purpose.
    If you try to follow every word, you will fall behind. But you can understand a lot.
    Try to focus on the speaker's purpose. The speaker's purpose guides the conversation.

Here are two examples. What is the speaker's purpose in each one?

1. Lois, no, please! Where are you going?

2. You leaving? Where are you going?
   a. He wants to go along.
   b. He doesn't want her to go.

STRATEGY 8: Predict what the speaker will say.
    Often you will think that spoken English is too fast to understand completely.
    You're right! It is too fast. Predicting will help you "listen faster." We have to predict
    words and ideas before we hear them.

Here are two examples. Can you predict the last part?
1. "I was very hungry...so I walked into the kitchen and opened the ...."

2. "Sharon studies all the time and she always gets excellent grades in school. She's so
   ...."

STRATEGY 9: Remember the meaning.
    Sometimes you will get discouraged about listening.
    That's normal — learning to listen takes a long time.
    To improve your listening ability, try to develop your memory. After you listen,
    pick a word or an expression or an idea that you want to remember.

Here are two examples. Are there any new words or expressions in these conversations?
Write them down.

1. A: What's the weather like there?   B: *Terrible. Rainy and bitter cold. Really nasty.*

   new word or expression : .... What does it mean? ....

2. A: How was the concert?   B: *Ah, so-so. They weren't really into it.*

   new word or expression : .... What does it mean? ....

Get Ready

Idea Preview

Look at each pair of items. Which do you prefer? Why?

a car

a bicycle

cordless telephone

speaker phone

a TV set

a book

an exercise bike

a walking machine

A   Here are some shopping situations.
Listen. Compare the items. Put a check next to the correct one.

1.

Which one has a clearer picture?

2.

Which one can store the most numbers?

3.
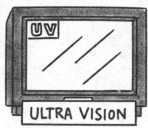
Which one is faster?

4.

Which one has more exercises?

B Listen. Which item do they prefer? Why do they prefer each item?
Circle the key ideas.

1. Televisions

Man:
a. Star One
b. Ultra Vision

   size
   sound
   price

Woman:
a. Star One
b. Ultra Vision

   size
   sound
   price

2. Telephones

Woman:
a. Sonic 2000
b. Pacific 4000

   extra features
   convenience
   price

Man:
a. Sonic 2000
b. Pacific 4000

   extra features
   convenience
   price

3. Bicycles

Man:
a. Trekker 1000
   (City Bike)
b. Streaker 9000
   (Racing Bike)

   convenience
   price
   power

Woman:
a. Trekker 1000
   (City Bike)
b. Streaker 9000
   (Racing Bike)

   convenience
   price
   power

4. Exercise Machines

Woman:
a. Super Body
   (Large)
b. Modern Life
   (Small)

   size
   variety
   power

Man:
a. Super Body
   (Large)
b. Modern Life
   (Small)

   size
   variety
   power

C Listen to these three people. They're trying to make a decision.
What would you do? Why?

LISTENING STRATEGY Try to understand the speaker's attitude.

1. University of Minnesota

key points:

University of Miami

key points:

2. study in the United States

key points:

study in Australia

key points:

3. work for Sybase

key points:

work for Sega

key points:

Listen again. What did they decide to do?

1. University of Minnesota

University of Miami

main reason:

2. study in the United States

study in Australia

main reason:

3. work for Sybase

work for Sega

main reason:

D Decide on a weekend plan with your partner.
First list two or more activities for each category.
Then choose one in each category.

OUTDOORS
a hike
windsurfing
....
....

SPORTS
a tennis match
a basketball game
....
....

ENTERTAINMENT
an action movie
a Shakespeare play
....
....

MUSIC
a concert
a country-western club
....
....

CULTURE
an exhibit on Egyptian art
a folk dance class
....
....

Now write your weekend schedule. Give reasons for your choices.

FRIDAY NIGHT:
6 pm _____
7 pm _____
8 pm _____
9 pm _____
10 pm _____
11 pm _____

SATURDAY AFTERNOON:
1 pm _____
2 pm _____
3 pm _____
4 pm _____

SATURDAY NIGHT:
5 pm _____
6 pm _____
7 pm _____

SUNDAY AFTERNOON:
1 pm _____
2 pm _____
3 pm _____
4 pm _____
5 pm _____
6 pm _____

Get Ready

Idea Preview

Which of these topics do you often talk about with your friends?

- sports
- holidays
- money
- crime
- work
- hobbies
- movies
- current news
- clothes
- gossip
- weather
- health
- sex
- school

Do you ever have arguments with people?
What topics do you sometimes argue about?

A Listen. What are they talking about? Number the topics.

HOBBIES

NATIONALITY

STUDYING ENGLISH

SHOPPING

SPORTS

SCHOOL DAYS

HEALTH

MOVIE STARS

THE WEATHER

WORK

A MEAL

B Listen. What is each argument about? Circle a, b, or c.

1.

   a. Bobby doesn't want to do his job now.
   b. Bobby's father doesn't want him to play basketball.
   c. Bobby wants his father to do his job.

2.

   a. She doesn't understand him.
   b. He hardly ever talks to her.
   c. She talks too much.

3.

   a. She borrowed her brother's Walkman.
   b. He didn't return his sister's Walkman.
   c. He broke his sister's Walkman.

4.

   a. He had a bad day.
   b. He doesn't ask about her feelings.
   c. He is not interested in her.

C Below are some idioms. An idiom is an expression that means more than the individual words. Here are some English idioms:

- He gets on my nerves. (He bothers me.)
- We really get along well. (We are good friends.)

LISTENING STRATEGY   Remember the meaning.

Close your books and listen. Can you get the general idea of the conversations?

Now look at the book. Listen again.
What does the speaker mean? Circle a, b, or c.

1. That's *the last straw*.

   a. He should always phone her.
   b. That's his final chance.
   c. He did that last night.

2. It's been *touch and go*.

   a. He feels bad most days.
   b. He wants to leave the hospital soon.
   c. The situation is sometimes good, sometimes bad.

3. I'm not *cut out for that*.

   a. This kind of work is not right for me.
   b. I'm a very good sales representative.
   c. My job is too dangerous.

4. I can't *make heads or tails out of it*.

   a. It isn't a very honest assignment.
   b. It's difficult for him to understand.
   c. It's an assignment that everyone must do.

5. I'm *burned out*.

   a. I don't have enough energy to do it.
   b. I'm very angry about the work.
   c. I don't have any time.

6. I couldn't *keep a straight face*.

   a. I tried to stop laughing, but I couldn't.
   b. I was very pleased because they tried so hard.
   c. I forgot to tell them my opinion.

P̲air A̲ctivity

D Partner 1, choose a number from 1 to 15. Partner 2, choose a topic, a or b.
Try to talk together for two minutes about that topic.

Example: neighbors
A: I have a lot of neighbors.
B: *Who's your favorite?*
A: Well, I really like ...

1
a. neighbors
b. a popular restaurant

2
a. a recent news story
b. a pet

3
a. first girlfriend/boyfriend
b. a popular TV show

4
a. the changing of the seasons
b. a best friend

5
a. transportation in this city
b. a family member

6
a. cars
b. what I think about this English class

7
a. environmental problems
b. a favorite movie

8
a. traveling
b. today's newspaper

9
a. sports
b. the cost of living

10
a. health
b. our English teacher

11
a. a next-door neighbor
b. ways of saving energy

12
a. first encounter with a foreigner
b. college entrance examinations

13
a. why I want (or don't want) a car
b. why ..... is an advanced country

14
a. how I relax
b. change of seasons in ......

15
a. the pet I'd like to have
b. video games

Now switch roles. Try again.

Get Ready

Idea Preview

Can you give directions to:

- the nearest restroom?
- the building exit?
- the school office?
- the coffee/drink machine?
- the nearest bus stop?

Language Preview

Do you know these expressions?

Can you tell me where the classroom is?
Can you tell me how to get to the classroom?
It's on the left.
It's at the end of the hall.
Go right at the stairs.

A Listen to these people asking for directions. Write the correct number next to the place.

1. men's room
2. drinking fountain
3. copy room
4. stairway
5. Audrey Clark's office
6. computer room

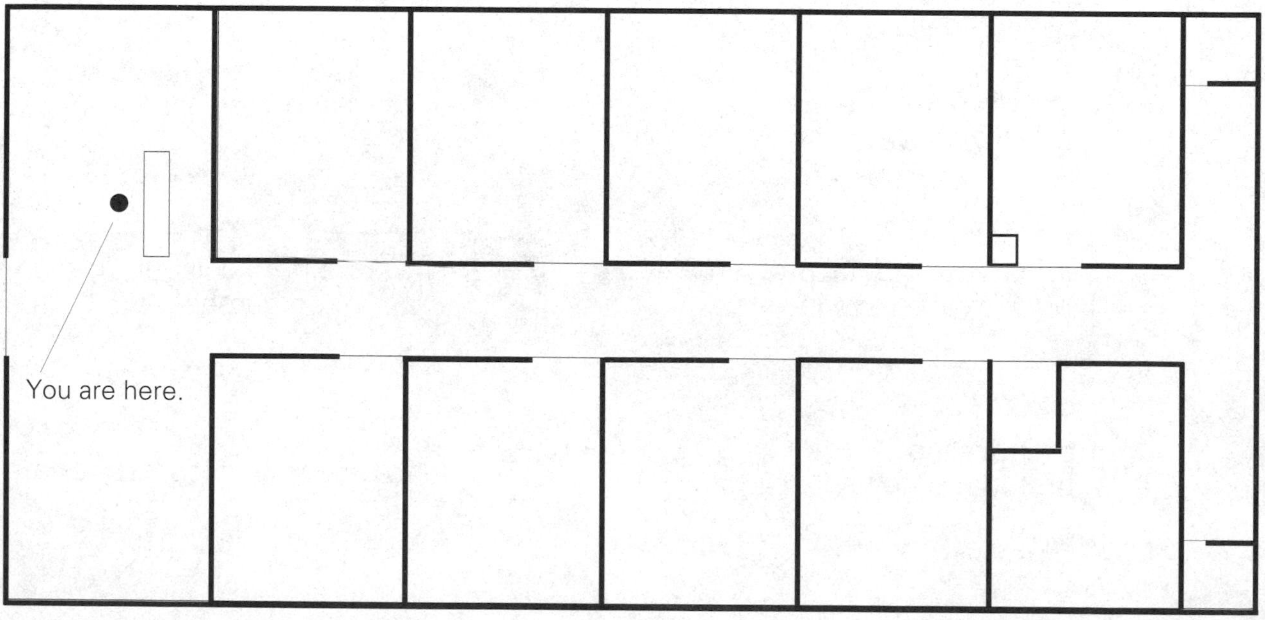

You are here.

B What is Washington, D.C., famous for?
Do you know these places?

The Capitol Building   The Smithsonian Museum
The Washington Monument   The White House

Listen to these tourists asking for directions.
Trace (→) the route to each place on the map.

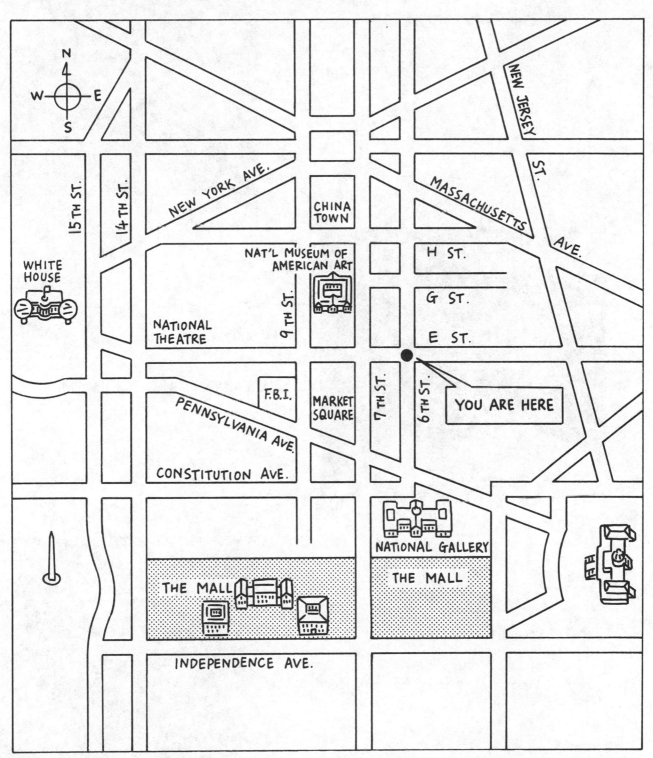

C Have you ever been lost? Where were you? What happened?
Listen to three people talking about getting lost.   What happened to them?

1. Janice

TRYING TO FIND

WHAT WAS THE PROBLEM?

2. Paul

TRYING TO FIND

WHAT WAS THE PROBLEM?

3. Sylvia

TRYING TO FIND

WHAT WAS THE PROBLEM?

P air A ctivity

D Choose a place on the map. Don't say the name. Give the directions.
Can your partner find that place?

Example:
A: Start at the Capitol Building. Go down Massachusetts
Avenue until you get to Connecticut Avenue.
B: *Go down Massachusetts Avenue... then what?*
A: Then turn right. You'll see it on your left side.

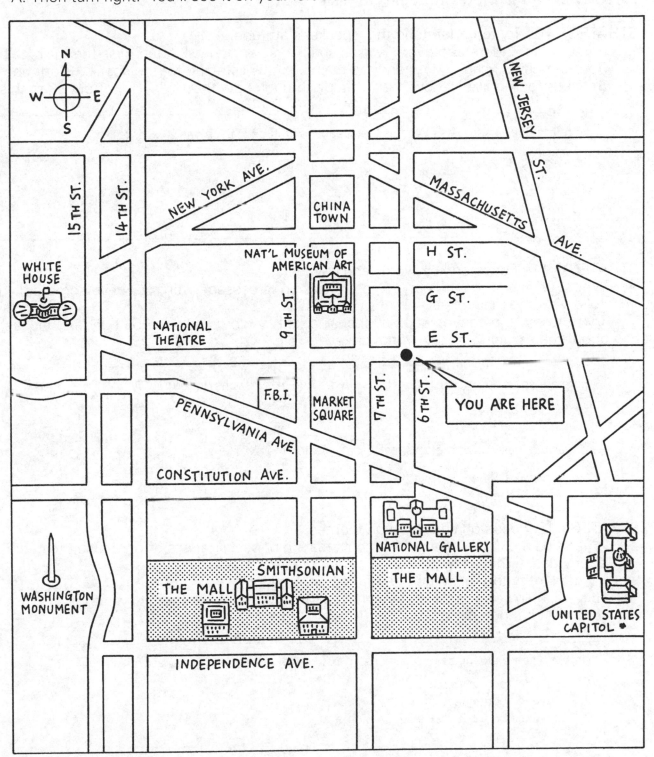

Let's review three more strategies for listening.

STRATEGY 10: Try to understand the speaker's attitude.

If you try to understand every word a speaker says, you will often miss the main point. Sometimes you can understand the main point by listening for the speaker's attitude. Speakers sometimes show their attitude through how they talk. Pay attention to this.

Here are three examples. What is the speaker's attitude in each one?

1. positive
2. negative
3. uncertain

a. ....   b. ....   c. ....

STRATEGY 11: Focus on key words and key facts.

When you are listening to a long conversation or passage, you may have some difficulty following the main ideas. That's normal.
Try to follow the conversation by focusing on key words. If you don't understand, ask about the meaning of key words or key facts.

Here are some examples of questions. What kind of questions do they ask?

1. ask about a word
2. ask about a fact

"I was at a party and I met this really sophisticated man..."

a. ....   b. ....   c. ....

STRATEGY 12: Focus on conversation themes.

When you are listening to a long conversation or passage, it is often difficult to catch every idea. That's OK.
Try to identify the main themes of the conversation.
This will help you keep up. If you have difficulty, ask about the theme of the conversation, not about words or details.

Here are some examples of questions. What kind of questions do they ask?

1. question about a word
2. question about a fact
3. question about the conversation theme

a. ....   b. ....   c. ....

Get Ready

Idea Preview

What would you say? Write a short response.

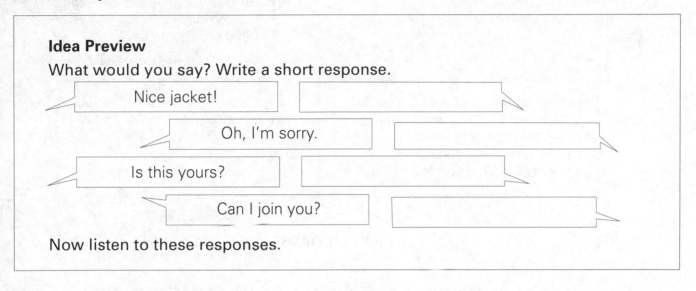

Now listen to these responses.

A   Here are some statements and requests.
Read each sentence. How would you respond?

Now listen. The speakers give polite responses.
What do they say? Write their POLITE responses.

1. Hey, that's a nice sweater!

polite
....

impolite
.... *about my clothes!*

2. Oh, no. I'm sorry.

polite
....

impolite
....

3. Would you like to go out for
   a coffee after class?

polite
....

impolite
....

4. Say, could I join you?

polite
....

impolite
.... *be alone.*

5. I wonder if you could lend
   me a few dollars?

polite
....

impolite
.... *money to anyone.*

6. Could you pick that up for me?

polite
....

impolite
.... *yourself.*

Listen again. These speakers give impolite responses.
What do they say? Write their IMPOLITE responses.

B Here are some difficult situations. Read each one.
Think about what you would say.

1.

> Your friend took a very important exam yesterday, but she failed it. She tells you the news. What would you say?

2.

> Your son is playing on a football team. It's very hard for him. He tells you that he's planning to quit tomorrow. What would you say?

3.

> Last week you sold your old car to a friend for $1,000. Today your friend tells you that the car is broken down and doesn't work at all. What would you say?

4.

> You lent your friend $20 last week. It seems he forgot about it. Today you see him in class. What would you say?

KEY WORDS

1.
• don't worry about it
• you'll do better...
• I knew you'd...

2.
• put in a lot of work
• It's up to you

3.
• cancel the deal
• refund your money
• tough luck

4.
• I was wondering...
• it's about time...

Now listen to Tom and Julie's responses. What is their response? Do you think they give friendly or unfriendly responses?

Tom   Julie

1. Your friend failed the test.

1	2	3	4	⑤
unfriendly				friendly

1	2	3	4	5
unfriendly				friendly

2. Your son wants to quit football.

1	2	3	4	5
unfriendly				friendly

1	2	3	4	5
unfriendly				friendly

3. The car broke down.

1	2	3	4	5
unfriendly				friendly

1	2	3	4	5
unfriendly				friendly

4. Your friend borrowed money

1	2	3	4	5
unfriendly				friendly

1	2	3	4	5
unfriendly				friendly

C What do you think of these company logos? Listen to Mike and Anne discussing the logos. Number the pictures. Then circle their opinions or reactions.

Try to understand the speaker's attitude.

1

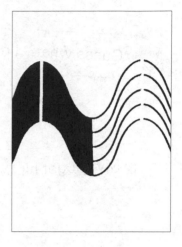

....

opinion
Mike: I like it.
      I hate it.
Anne: It's interesting.
      It's confusing.

....

opinion
Mike: It's funny.
      It's unclear.
      It's silly.
Anne: It's nice.
      It's perfect.
      It doesn't fit.

....

opinion
Mike: It's attractive.
      It's smooth.
Anne: I like it.
      It's OK.

6

....

opinion
Mike: It's different.
      It's typical.
      It's old-fashioned.
Anne: It's all right.
      It's not so special.
      It's fresh.

....

opinion
Mike: I sort of like it.
      It's powerful.
      It's unique.
Anne: It's striking.
      It's active.
      It's different.

....

opinion
Mike: It doesn't fit.
      It's really attractive.
Anne: It's like a flower.
      It's pleasant.
      It's nice..

Now listen again. Write their opinions.

Pair Activity

D Work in pairs or groups. Pick a Statement card. Read the statement.
How many responses can you think of? Try to think of at least 3 responses.

Guess what? I'm getting married next week.

Can I borrow some money?

My cat got hit by a car.

Would you like to go out for coffee after class?

Here's a glass of orange juice for you.

Hey, that's a great haircut!

I need a ride home.

I'd better be going.

I just passed my English test.

My computer broke yesterday.

I just moved to a new apartment

Do you like my new T-shirt?

Get Ready

Idea Preview

How have you changed in the past year? Think of two ways.

I have ....

What do you think will happen in the future...

concerning fashion?	I think ....
concerning music?	I think ....
concerning marriage?	I think ....
concerning world population?	I think ....

Think of at least one thing.

Language Preview

Do you know these expressions?

increasing   decreasing   rapidly   definitely   percentage   more nutritious
healthier   more efficient   more convenient   less fun   much easier

A   Listen to these situations. What's changing?
Draw an arrow -- (↑) (↓) (→) -- to show how it's changing.

1.
.... World population

.... Population in
         industrialized countries

.... Population in
         developing countries

2.
.... Age of people when
        they first get married

.... Age of men when they
        first get married

.... Age of women when
        they first get married

3.
.... Life expectancy of people
        in most countries

.... Life expectancy of men
        in most countries

.... Life expectancy of women
        in most countries

B Look at each graph. Complete the missing information in the boxes [ ].

1. World population

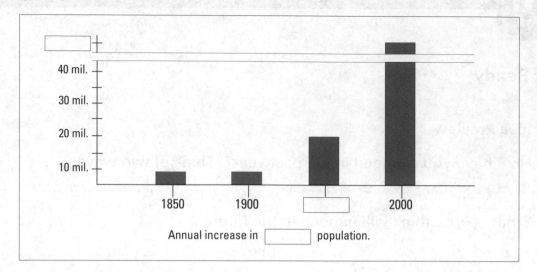

Annual increase in [ ] population.

2. Percentage of people married at age 24

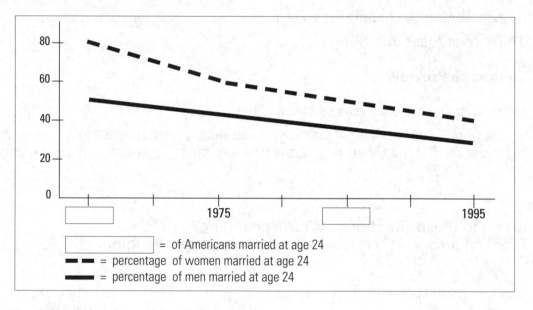

[ ] = of Americans married at age 24
- - - = percentage of women married at age 24
——— = percentage of men married at age 24

3. Life expectancy

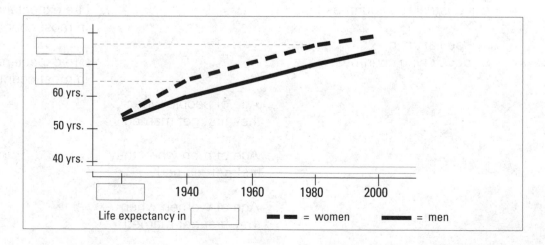

Life expectancy in [ ]   - - - = women   ——— = men

C Imagine the future. How will fashion change? Jobs? Health?
Listen to these experts' opinions. Write short notes as you listen.

LISTENING STRATEGY Focus on key words and key facts.

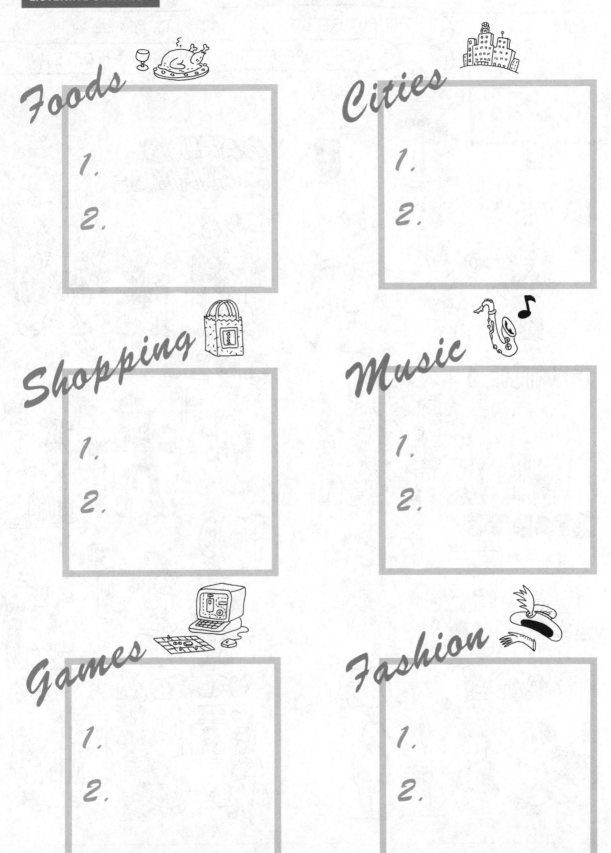

Foods

1.

2.

Cities

1.

2.

Shopping

1.

2.

Music

1.

2.

Games

1.

2.

Fashion

1.

2.

D Choose 5 topics from the list below. What do you think the future trend will be? Make two sentences about each topic.

ADVICE

Get Ready

Idea Preview

Who would you ask for advice about:

marriage partners?
problems with your parents?
problems at school?
health problems?

Language Preview

You should...
Why don't you...?
How about trying...?

A Here are some simple problems.
What's the problem? What's the advice? Write short notes.

1. Jenny's problem

....

Dan's advice

....

2. Wendell's problem

....

Jill's advice

....

3. Sandy's problem

....

Tim's advice

....

4. Sue's problem

....

Dad's advice

....

5. Biff's problem

....

Linda's advice

....

6. Ana's problem

....

James's advice

....

B Here are some social problems.
Listen to each speaker. What's the problem? Circle a, b, or c.

Miss Understanding

I'm a Japanese American but ...

1.
a. People don't think she's really American.
b. She wants to return to Japan.
c. She doesn't speak English very well.

3.
a. His fiancee wants him to change his religion.
b. Her parents think he's a foreigner.
c. Her parents want him to change his religion.

2.
a. She doesn't want to go to her friends' house for dinner.
b. She thinks her friends feel sorry for her.
c. She would like to invite her friends to her house.

4.
a. He always spends too much money in restaurants.
b. He didn't have enough money to pay the bill.
c. His friends were unfair to him.

HINT
First read the questions and the key words. Then listen without looking at your book.

KEY WORDS

1.
• ancestors
• I feel strange..

2.
• I'm single
• married friends
• insult

3.
• fiancee
• get married
• give up

4.
• upset
• dinner was on me
• it ruined my...

C Now listen to Miss Understanding's advice about the problems. What does she think? Circle a, b, or c. Then decide: do you agree with the advice?

LISTENING STRATEGY   Focus on conversation themes.

Miss Understanding

I understand your problem...

1. Rude questions

a. Say, "I'm from the United States. Where are you from?"

b. Don't worry about it. They're trying to be polite.

c. Tell them it's a rude question. Don't answer it.

   Do you agree? ....

2. Single woman, married friends

a. Invite them to your house.

b. Stop visiting them.

c. Tell them how you feel.

   Do you agree? ....

3. International relationships.

a. Try to persuade her parents.

b. Talk to your fiancee very honestly.

c. Change your religion.

   Do you agree? ....

4. A bad restaurant experience.

a. Don't invite your friends anymore.

b. Ask your friends to give you some money.

c. Next time choose the food and drinks yourself.

   Do you agree? ....

KEY WORDS

1.	2.	3.	4.
• rude	• selfish	• can be a	• nothing you can
• have contact with	• give the impression	headache	do about it
• show their interest	• for a change	• talk frankly	• decline your
• be offended		• respect	invitation

D Choose one problem. What advice would you give?

MISS
UNDERSTANDING

Q: I'm having a problem. I've just moved to the United States and my English is not very good.
When I speak, I think Americans are making fun of me. This makes me very nervous, so I don't want to try to make any American friends. I only stay around people from my own country. What should I do?

YOUR ADVICE

Q: I'm having a problem. I've just married a wonderful man and after we got married we moved into his parents' house. Before we were married, we were both very happy, but now we are miserable!!! His mother (my mother-in-law) is always complaining that I don't do enough around the house and she criticizes my cooking. I have a full-time job and I think she wants me to quit my job and spend more time at home. But I don't want to spend more time around her! What can I do??

YOUR ADVICE

Q: I'm having a problem. Three years ago I bought a beautiful home in the countryside. It was very peaceful and quiet — until last year. Last summer, new neighbors moved into the house next to mine. They have three large dogs that bark all the time, and last week, they bought two ponies for their children! Now my yard smells and I feel like I live in a zoo. What can I do?

YOUR ADVICE

Now write an original letter about a new problem.
Give it to your partner. Can your partner give you advice?

A Topics (15 points)
Listen. What is the topic or main idea of each conversation?
Circle a, b, or c.

1. a. what she bought
   b. what she will buy
   c. how much she spent

2. a. where he lives
   b. where he comes from
   c. where he is moving

3. a. an actress
   b. a friend
   c. a boss

4. a. their schedule
   b. their next meeting
   c. their work

5. a. a date
   b. an appointment
   c. a medical problem

B Reasons. (15 points)
Listen. Why did they choose each item? Circle the reasons.

1. a. he needs a new car
   b. he needs a lot of space
   c. he doesn't have any equipment

2. a. she doesn't have enough money
   b. she's very hungry
   c. she bought it for him

3. a. it's not too big
   b. it's not so sweet
   c. it's not very expensive

4. a. they're inexpensive
   b. they're comfortable
   c. they're new

5. a. it's cheaper
   b. it's more convenient
   c. it's closer

C Responses. (15 points)
Listen. What would be the best response? Circle your answer.

1. a. Thank you.
   b. No, thank you.

2. a. Sure.
   b. That's OK.

3. a. Oh, sure. That would be great.
   b. Yes, please.

4. a. This way, please.
   b. Sure.

5. a. No, thanks.
   b. Sorry, I can't.

6. a. Just one.
   b. Sure. Here you are.

D Directions. (15 points)
Listen to the people asking for directions. Write the correct number next to the place.

1. men's room
4. Audrey Clark's office

2. copy room
5. computer room

3. stairway

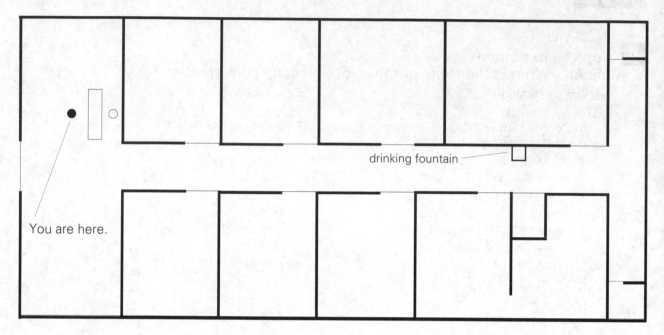

You are here.

drinking fountain

E Choices (20 points)
Listen. What choices are they trying to make? Circle the correct answer.

1. a. two universities
   b. two professors
   c. two courses

2. a. places to travel
   b. places to study English
   c. places to have a good time

3. a. which job is better
   b. which city is better·
   c. which company is better

F Advice (20 points)
Listen. What is the problem? Circle your answer.

1. a. She doesn't have any friends.
   b. She wants to move to France.
   c. She can't learn French easily.

2. a. His girlfriend is a better musician.
   b. His father doesn't like his girlfriend.
   c. Her father doesn't want her to marry him.

3. a. She has too many children.
   b. The children are noisy.
   c. The children are not patient.

Now listen to some advice. What does the speaker say? Circle your answer.

1. a. Leave France as soon as possible.
   b. Speak English as much as possible.
   c. Keep trying to learn French.

2. a. Talk to her father directly.
   b. Stop visiting her father.
   c. Ask her to talk to him.

3. a. Talk to the children's parents.
   b. Tell the children to be quiet .
   c. Be more patient with the children.

What is your score for this review test? ⬚ / ⬚ %
100 points

Self Evaluation

Look at pages 18 , 31, 51, and 64.
Which strategies are helping you listen better?

....
....
....

Which strategies do you want to try using more?

....
....
....